THIS CANDLEWICK BOOK BELONGS TO:

_____

_____

_____

_____

Greater horseshoe bat
(Rhinolophus ferrumequinum)

Greater bulldog bat
(Noctilio leporinus)

White fruit bats
(Ectophylla alba)

Common vampire bat
(Desmodus rotundus)

Hardwickes mouse-tailed bat
(Rhinopoma hardwickei)

Spotted bat
(Euderma maculatum)

Bats are the only mammals that can really fly,
and flight has made them very successful.
There are more than nine hundred species, living in
almost every habitat from subarctic tundra to
tropical forests and deserts. Birds may rule the air
by day, but bats are the monarchs of the night.

This book is about one of the pipistrelle bats.
Pipistrelles are found around the world,
from North America to Africa, Europe,
Asia, and Australia.

Indian flying foxes
(Pteropus giganteus)

For Henry Venner Woodcock and his big brothers,
Alfie and Thomas
N. D.

For Ailsa
S. F.-D.

Text copyright © 2001 by Nicola Davies
Illustrations copyright © 2001 by Sarah Fox-Davies

First U.S. paperback edition 2004

The Library of Congress has cataloged the hardcover edition as follows:

Davies, Nicola.
Bat loves the night / Nicola Davies ; illustrated by Sarah Fox-Davies. —1st U.S. ed.
p. cm.
Summary: Bat wakes up, flies into the night, uses the echoes of her
voice to navigate, hunts for her supper, and returns to her roost to feed her baby.

ISBN 978-0-7636-1202-3 (hardcover)
1. Bats — Juvenile fiction. [1. Bats—Fiction.] I. Fox-Davies, Sarah, ill. II. Title.
PZ10.3.D2865 Bat 2001
[E]—dc21 00-066681

ISBN 978-0-7636-2438-5 (paperback)

19 20 21 22 SWT 30

Printed in Dongguan, Guangdong, China

This book was typeset in Cochin and Sanvito.
The illustrations were done in watercolor and pencil.

Candlewick Press
99 Dover Street
Somerville, Massachusetts 02144

visit us at www.candlewick.com

BAT
LOVES
THE
NIGHT

Nicola Davies

illustrated by Sarah Fox-Davies

CANDLEWICK PRESS

Bat is waking,
upside down as usual,
hanging by her toenails.

Her beady eyes open.
Her pixie ears twitch.

She shakes her
thistledown fur.

She unfurls her wings,
made of skin so fine the finger bones
inside show through.

The pipistrelle bat's
body is no bigger than
your thumb.

A bat's wing is its
arm and hand.
Four extra-long fingers
support the skin of the wing.

7

Bats' toes are shaped like hooks,
so it's no effort for a bat to hang
upside down.

Now she unhooks her toes
and drops into black space.
With a sound like a tiny umbrella
opening, she flaps her wings.

Bat is flying.

Out!

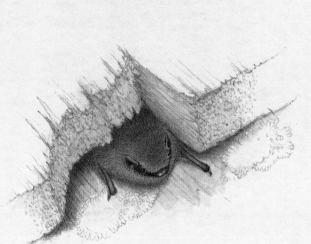

Out under the broken tile
into the nighttime garden.

Over bushes, under trees,
between fence posts,
through the tangled hedge
she swoops untouched.
Bat is at home in the darkness
as a fish is in the water.
She doesn't need to see —
she can hear where she is going.

Bats can see. But in the dark, good ears are
more useful than eyes.

Bat shouts as she flies, louder
than a hammer blow, higher than a
squeak. She beams her voice around her
like a flashlight, and the echoes come
singing back. They carry a sound picture
of all her voice has touched.
Listening hard, Bat can hear every
detail, the smallest twigs, the
shape of leaves.

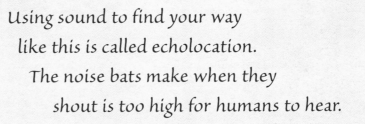

Using sound to find your way
like this is called echolocation.
The noise bats make when they
shout is too high for humans to hear.

Gliding and fluttering
back and forth,
she shouts her torch of
sound among the trees,
listening for her supper.

All is still. . . .

15

Then a fat moth takes flight below her.

Bat plunges, fast as blinking, and grabs it in her open mouth.

But the moth's pearly scales are moon-dust slippery. It slithers from between her teeth.

Bat dives, nets it with a wing tip, scoops it to her mouth.

This time she bites hard.
Its wings fall away, like the
wrapper from a candy.
In a moment the moth is eaten.
Bat sneezes.
The dusty scales got up her nose.

A bat can eat dozens of big moths
in a single night — or thousands of tiny
flies, gnats, and mosquitoes.

Most species of bats eat
insects, but there are some
that eat fruit, fish, frogs,
even blood!

Hunting time has run out.
The dark will soon be gone.
In the east, the sky is getting light.
It's past Bat's bedtime.

The place where bats sleep in the day is called a roost.
It can be in a building, a cave, or a tree, so long as it's dry and safe.

She flies to the roof in the last shadows
and swoops in under the broken tile.

Inside, there are squeakings.
Fifty hungry batlings hang in a huddle,
hooked to a rafter by oversized feet.
Bat lands and pushes in among them,
toes first, upside down again.

Baby bats can't fly.
Sometimes mother bats carry their babies when
they go out, but mostly the babies stay behind in the roost
and crowd together to keep warm.

Bat knows her
baby's voice, and
calls to it.

The velvet scrap
batling climbs aboard
and clings to Bat's fur
by its coat-hanger feet.

Wrapped in her
leather wings, the
baby suckles
Bat's milk.

Baby bats drink mother's milk until
they learn to fly at a few weeks old.
Then they can leave the roost
at night to find their own food.

25

Outside, the birds are singing.
The flowers turn their faces to the sun.
But inside the roof hole,
the darkness stays.
Bat dozes with her batling,
waiting.

Bats are nocturnal. That means they rest by day
and come out at night to search for food.

When the tide of night rises again,
Bat will wake and plunge
into the blackness, shouting.

Bat loves the night.

Index

Look up the pages to find
out about all these batty things.
Don't forget to look at both
kinds of words —
this kind and
this kind.

Mexican freetail bat

(Tadarida brasiliensis)

Nicola Davies loves to be out under the stars, watching bats, and is lucky enough to live in a cottage with pipistrelles in its roof. She enjoys learning about mammals of all kinds, and her studies have led her around the world. Nicola Davies is the author of *Big Blue Whale*, *One Tiny Turtle*, *Ice Bear*, and *Surprising Sharks*.

Sarah Fox-Davies has illustrated many picture books for children, including *Walk with a Wolf* by Janni Howker, and *Snow Bears* by Martin Waddell. Sarah Fox-Davies says that while she was painting the illustrations for this book, a pipistrelle bat flew into her studio—and right onto her desk!